WHAT HAPPENED AFTER WORLD WAR II?

History Book for Kids
Children's War & Military Books

BABY PROFESSOR
EDUCATION KIDS

Speedy Publishing LLC

40 E. Main St. #1156

Newark, DE 19711

www.speedypublishing.com

Copyright 2017

In this book, we're going to talk about the events that happened after World War II. So, let's get right to it!

When World War II was coming to a close, the United States, Britain, and the Soviet Union leaders met to discuss the future of Germany and its allies. At that time Germany had already surrendered, but Japan had not.

POTSDAM CONFERENCE GROUP PORTRAIT

WHAT WAS THE POTSDAM CONFERENCE?

The Potsdam Conference was attended by the three largest of the Allied Powers. These important leaders were:

- United States President Harry S. Truman
- Britain's Prime Minister, Winston Churchill, and, later in the meeting, Clement Attlee, who was Churchill's successor
- The Soviet Union's leader, Joseph Stalin

There were many goals for this meeting, which took place from July 17 through August 2nd of 1945.

A WOMAN LABORER DURING WORLD WAR 2

THE GERMAN ECONOMY

The leaders discussed actions needed to stabilize the German economy. They wanted the German people to focus on agricultural and nonmilitary industries. They would decentralize the institutions that had managed and controlled Germany's economy during the Nazi reign.

A COUNCIL OF FOREIGN MINISTERS

They created a Council of Foreign Ministers, which included the countries represented at the Potsdam Conference and also included China and France.

POTSDAM CONFERENCE

GERMAN TROOPS

POLICIES FOR THE GERMAN MILITARY

They also discussed establishing a Control Council run by the Allied Powers for the management of Germany, especially the management of Germany's military.

This council had to be in complete agreement in order for policies to be determined. Later on, this need for a unanimous vote caused problems for approving policies.

TRIALS FOR GERMAN WAR CRIMINALS

There was also the matter of how to send war criminals to trial and how they should be punished for the crimes they had committed during the war.

358-S

DEMAND FOR UNCONDITIONAL SURRENDER

Most of the discussion centered around topics related to Europe, but they also demanded that Japan state that they were "unconditionally surrendering." The leaders did not discuss this publicly, but they had decided that Japan could keep their emperor.

BOUNDARIES BETWEEN COUNTRIES

Stalin wanted to discuss the final borders of Poland and Germany, but those decisions were put off until the official peace treaty. Some of the land transfers that Stalin suggested were approved.

While the conference was going on, President Truman received news that the atomic bomb test had been successful.

HARRY TRUMAN

WINSTON CHURCHILL AND HARRY TRUMAN

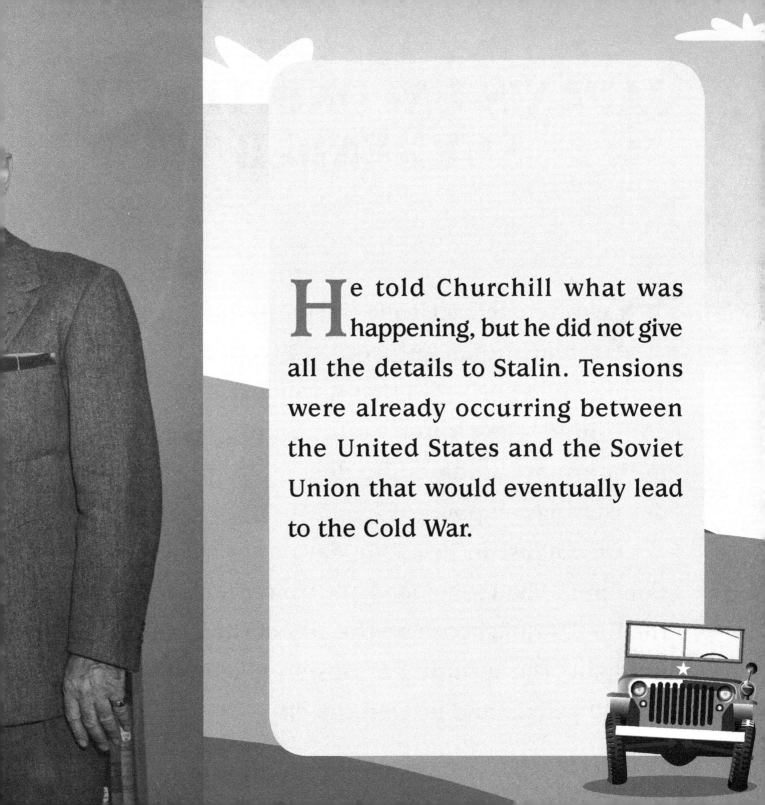

He told Churchill what was happening, but he did not give all the details to Stalin. Tensions were already occurring between the United States and the Soviet Union that would eventually lead to the Cold War.

JAPAN'S UNCONDITIONAL SURRENDER

Despite the fact that Germany had admitted defeat, Japan refused to give up. President Truman had been told that if the war in the Pacific continued, the United States would lose up to a million more soldiers. He decided to use the new devastating weapon.

On August 6, just four days after the Potsdam Conference had concluded, the United States dropped the first atomic bomb on the city of Hiroshima in Japan. The resulting explosion killed over 80,000 people and leveled the city.

Many thousands more people would die of the exposure to radiation over the coming days and years. However, Japan still didn't surrender.

Three days later, the United States dropped a second bomb on the city of Nagasaki. Another 40,000 Japanese people were killed. One week later, Hirohito, Japan's emperor announced the unconditional surrender of the Japanese people.

WAR CRIMES

After the war was over, the Allied Powers determined that some of the actions during the war were so terrible that those leaders must be punished. Many of the leaders in both Germany and Japan were tried in court, convicted, and executed. Some Nazi leaders killed themselves at the end of the war and others escaped and hid.

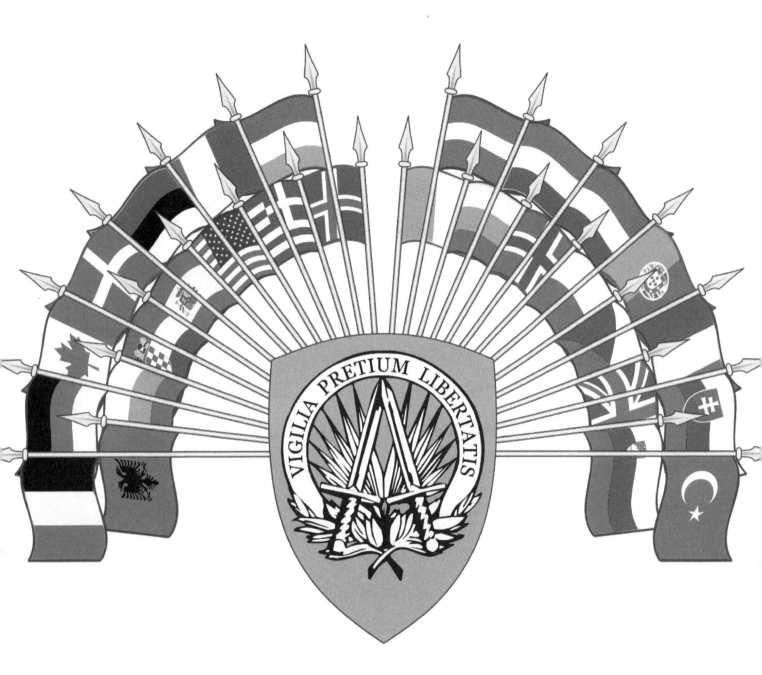

GREATER COAT OF ARMS OF SUPREME
HEADQUARTERS ALLIED POWERS EUROPE

Although both sides had killed their enemies during the war, there are certain types of actions that are considered to be beyond the international rules of what should be done, even within the context of war. For example, the killing of the Jewish people during the Holocaust was a war crime as well as a crime against humanity.

GERMAN WAR CRIMES

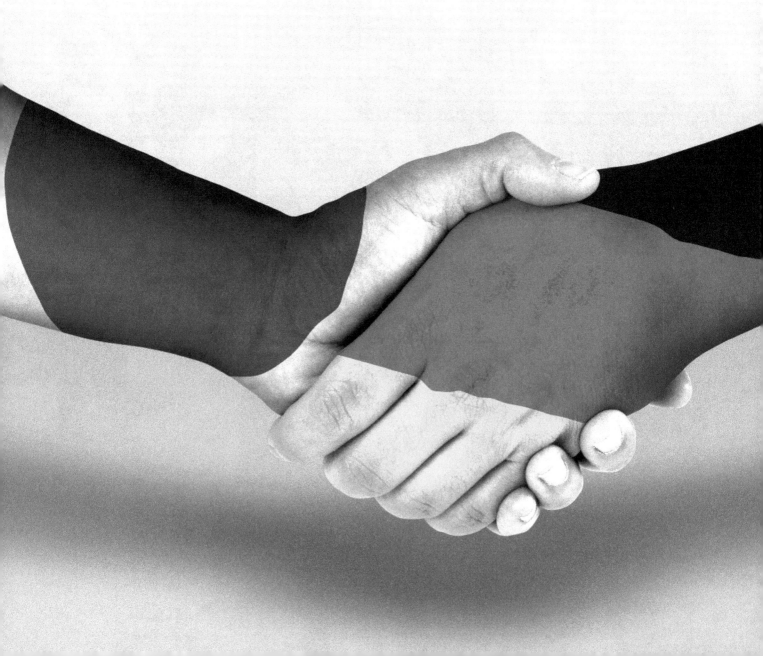

NEW BORDERS ESTABLISHED AFTER THE WAR

Germany and its ally Japan had taken over many countries in Europe as well as in Eastern Asia during World War II. Now that the war was over, the borders and the governments of those countries needed to be re-established.

EUROPE

In the western section of Europe, the countries were able to maintain their previous governments and their previous borders. Germany was divided into west and east sections. In addition to taking control of the eastern section of Germany as had been determined during the Potsdam conference, the Soviet Union took control over much of Eastern Europe where they had battled the Germans during World War II.

EUROPE
ATLANTIC OCEAN
ICELAND
IRELAND
UNITED KINGDOM
NORTH SEA
NORWAY
SWEDEN
FINLAND
RUSSIA
DENMARK
BALTIC SEA
ESTONIA
LATVIA
LITHUANIA
BELARUS
NETHERLANDS
BELGIUM
GERMANY
POLAND
UKRAINE
CZECH REPUBLIC
SLOVAKIA
AUSTRIA
HUNGARY
ROMANIA
MOLDOVA
FRANCE
SWITZERLAND
SLOVENIA
CROATIA
BOSNIA
SERBIA
BULGARIA
BLACK SEA
ITALY
ADRIATIC SEA
MONTENEGRO
ALBANIA
MAKEDONIA
GREECE
TURKEY
CYPRUS
SPAIN
PORTUGAL
MEDITERRANEAN SEA

FLAG OF SOVIET UNION

Europe was split almost in half, with the countries aligned with the United States on the west and the countries on the east overtaken by the Soviet Union. Italy had been on the opposite side in World War II, but became aligned with the United States after the war. The Soviet Union, which was once an ally of the United States, was becoming an enemy and freedom in Europe was threatened.

JAPAN AND EASTERN ASIA

The United States and the other Allied Powers took control over Japan after the war. General Douglas A. MacArthur was in charge of this effort as Japan's economic, political, and military systems were reformed.

DOUGLAS A. MACARTHUR

WAR FLAG OF THE IMPERIAL JAPANESE ARMY

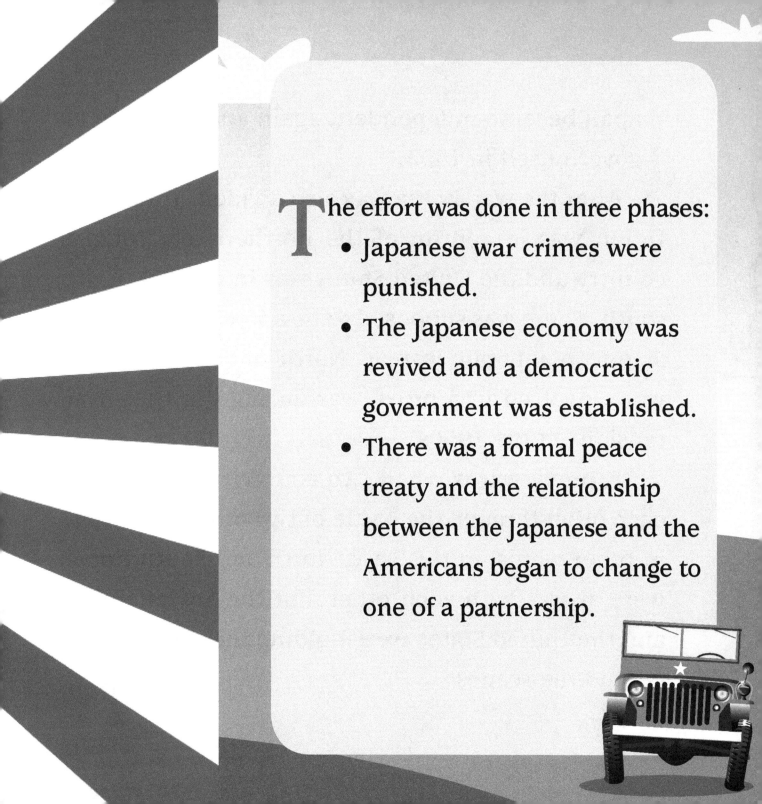

The effort was done in three phases:
- Japanese war crimes were punished.
- The Japanese economy was revived and a democratic government was established.
- There was a formal peace treaty and the relationship between the Japanese and the Americans began to change to one of a partnership.

Japan became independent again and was able to govern itself in 1952.

After the war, Korea was also divided. The Soviet Union was in control of the northern part of the country and the United States was in control of the south. There was supposed to be a free election held at one point, but instead North and South Korea were involved in a proxy war during the Cold War tensions of the 1950s.

A proxy war is when two countries are fighting each other through the battle of two other countries. In other words, in this case, North and South Korea were at war with each other, but the Soviet Union and the United States were holding the power behind the scenes.

NORTH KOREA

SOUTH KOREA

Military Demarcation Line

Demilitarized Zone (DMZ)

2nd Tunnel

1st Tunnel

3rd Tunnel

4th Tunnel

h Parallel

80,000,000 CHINESE COMMUNISTS WHO INHABIT
THOUSANDS OF SQUARE MILES OF NORTHERN CHINA

There was unrest in the huge country of China as well. A civil war had started before World War II and after World War II the fighting began again.

The war was fought between the communists and their enemies the nationalists. The nationalists lost and escaped to Taiwan. Communism had now spread to the most populated country worldwide.

HOW WAS GERMANY DIVIDED?

After the war, the Allied Powers divided Germany into two different parts—East and West. The western part of the nation was occupied by and controlled by the British, the United States, and France.

MAP OF GERMANY

STATE ARMS OF GERMAN DEMOCRATIC REPUBLIC

As soon as things stabilized, West Germany was established as a new democracy. The eastern part of the country was occupied and managed by the Soviet Union.

However, the Soviet Union didn't allow East Germany to become independent or establish a democratic form of government. The capital city of Germany, Berlin, was divided into west and east sections as well.

THE MARSHALL PLAN

Large sections of Europe had been destroyed during the war. Roads as well as bridges and many buildings had been reduced to rubble. The government of the US gave over $13 billion dollars in aid to Europe after World War II.

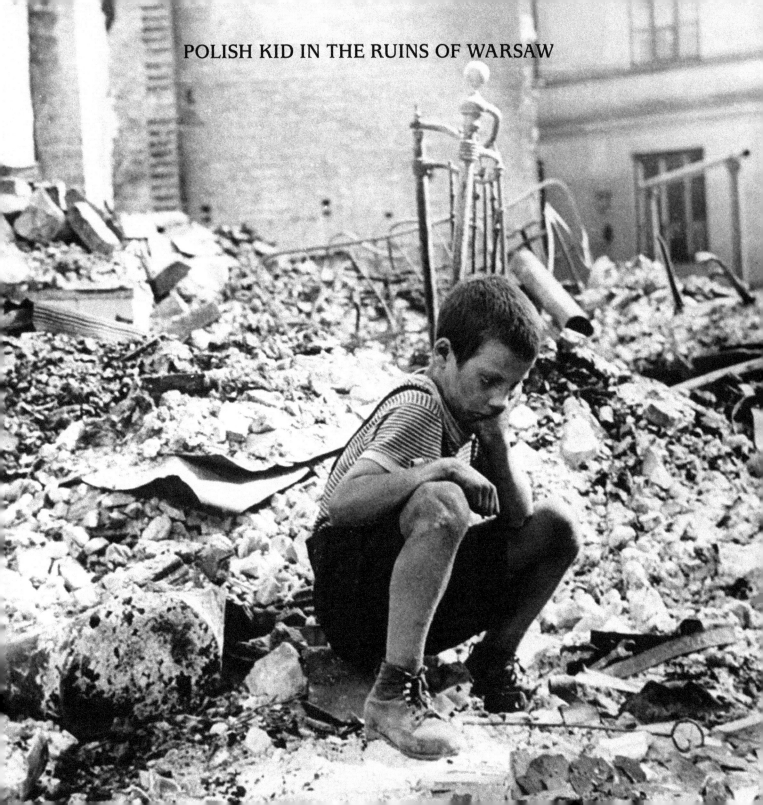

POLISH KID IN THE RUINS OF WARSAW

This policy was known as the Marshall Plan after a Virginia military leader named George C. Marshall who persuaded other leaders that it was the right thing to do.

The United States became very concerned about the spreading of communism. The leaders in the US wanted the countries of Europe to become stable and rebuild quickly so their governments would not be susceptible to communism.

BERLIN WALL

THE BERLIN WALL

In 1961, the East Germans built a wall dividing the city of Berlin. It started out as a fence but eventually was a tall, concrete wall. The communist leaders of East Germany didn't want people to go over to the West Berlin side. People wanted to cross over to West Germany because the government there was democratic and they would have more freedom.

Soldiers on the East German side would shoot to kill anyone who attempted to get over the Berlin Wall. The wall was there for 28 years. Then, in 1989 the people of Europe began to protest against the communist leadership. The wall was torn down and the two sides of Germany were joined again in 1990 under a democratic government.

BERLIN WALL NOW

STALIN, ROOSEVELT AND CHURCHILL

SUMMARY

After World War II, the Allied Powers decided how the countries of Germany and Japan should be rebuilt. Many of the leaders in Germany and Japan were brought to trial and convicted for their war crimes. The United States gave billions of dollars of aid to countries in Europe so they could rebuild.

The US also helped to rebuild Japan. The threat to the world before World War II had been Nazi Germany. At that time, the Soviet Union had been aligned with Britain and the United States to fight against Hitler. However, tensions between the United States and the Soviet Union started to build as communism began to spread. The stage was set for the Cold War.

Now that you know more about what happened after World War II, you may want to find out more about what events led up to World War II in the Baby Professor book Why Did Hitler Hate the Jews?

Visit

BABY PROFESSOR
EDUCATION KIDS

www.BabyProfessorBooks.com

to download Free Baby Professor eBooks
and view our catalog of new and exciting
Children's Books

CPSIA information can be obtained
at www.ICGtesting.com
Printed in the USA
LVHW060713280420
654650LV00011B/284